Tie a Wish™ with Bracelets

Easy and Fun Chinese Knotting

by

D. M. Chen & Michelle Sun

STORYROBINBOOKS

California, USA

ISBN 978-1-937489-01-4

Library of Congress Control Number:
2011940197

Text copyright © 2011 D. M. Chen
Tutorial Photographs by Michelle Sun
Illustrations by R. R. Jan
Edited by Carol Collins
Courtesy artworks by Jau-Tzong Yang and Helen Yu

Printed and bound in China

D. M. Chen:
To my mom, for all her
ethereal inspiration.

Michelle Sun:
To all my teachers, who have taught me the
art of Chinese knotting.

Table of Contents

Chapter 1 Introduction – Speaking in Knots   1

Chapter 2 The Art of Chinese Knotting   8

Chapter 3 Basic Techniques   10

Chapter 4 Tools, Materials, and the Basic Knot   12

Chapter 5 Simplicity   15
Double Knot
Helix Knot
Simplicity Bracelet _____
Creativity at Work

Chapter 6 Peace   20
Peace Knot
Peace Bracelet _____
Creativity at Work

Chapter 7 Wealth   30
Double-Coin Knot
Wealth Bracelet _____
Creativity at Work

Chapter 8 Friendship   35
Wheel Knot
Hand-in-Hand Friendship Bracelet _____
Creativity at Work

Chapter 9   Health   40

  Snake Knot

  Health Bracelet ————————————

  Creativity at Work

Chapter 10   Wisdom   45

  Button Knot

  Wisdom Bracelet ———————

  Creativity at Work

Chapter 11   Blessings   51

  Cloverleaf Knot

  Count-Your-Blessings Bracelet ———————

  Creativity at Work

Chapter 12   Luck   59

  Lucky Knot

  Lucky Flower Knot

  Lucky Bracelet ————————————

  Creativity at Work

Chapter 13 Tips on Creating Your Own Bracelets   69

Chapter 1

Introduction - Speaking in Knots

Sometimes it is not bad to be tongue tied.

Long ago in China, a man named Cangjie was responsible for keeping track of his village's population, assets and events. As the number of things he needed to track increased, he had a hard time remembering everything.

Soon, he began mixing the livestock population with the number of god worship ceremonies. And then, he confused the number of lambs with the amount of rice that was supposed to be in storage for the winter. "Oh no!" thought Cangjie, "I must stop making such errors."

Cangjie thought and thought until "Bingo!" - he found a solution. He twisted bark and plant leaves into cords, then tied knots to help him memorize things. For example, big knots represented large items, and small knots signified small things. Knot shapes and colors provided additional layers of meaning.

Cangjie's knots served him well until the village grew once again. Soon, he had more things to record than he had ways to knot. One day Cangjie saw three people arguing in an intersection. One person insisted that they should go east, for there would be a troupe of antelopes. Another person wanted to head north, saying that not far there would be deer. The third person said two fighting tigers were ahead of them in the west, and they shouldn't miss the opportunity to hunt injured tigers.

Cangjie was curious and asked how they knew all of this great information. The hunters pointed to animal footprints in the ground.

Cangjie, now inspired, thought, "Why don't I follow the animals' example and carve images of the knots?" Thus, Chinese characters emerged.

The Chinese continued to tie knots even after they invented writing with brush and paper. Knots became symbolic decorations for clothes, as well as ways to wear their favorite gem - jade.

7

Chapter 2

The Art of Chinese Knotting

With one piece of string, you can tie many different knots in unique combinations to create thousands of artworks. Each symmetrical Chinese knot creation is both beautiful and symbolic.

One string many artworks

8

A well designed Chinese knot
is truly a piece of art. The knot should
be neat and even. The color combinations
should complement the design. Will you need
lots of work to achieve that? No, you will see
improvements after each knot that you tie.

***Practice
makes
perfect***

Chapter 3
Basic Techniques

Traditionally, Chinese knotting has two major steps:

tying   **tightening**

In general, it is best to tighten while tying. Proper tightening determines the final shape of your design. In fact, if you remove unnecessary slack while tying a knot, the final tightening will be minimal.

Tightening Steps:

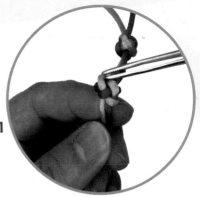

1. Study the loose loop that needs tightening. Wiggle the cord to trace the path from its origin to where it leads.

2. Gently and evenly pull the cord along its path.

3. Pull the cord bit by bit. Don't fully tighten the cord if other parts are still very loose. Strive for even tension among all cords. If one cord is overly tight, it might prevent later adjustment of the other loops.

Just as Goldilocks would say, "not too tight, not too loose, just right."

Chapter 4   Tools, Materials, and the Basic Knot

Scissors for trimming cords.

Rulers for measuring cords. This book uses centimeters, but it includes measurements in inches rounded up to the nearest 1/4 or 1/2.

Pins or adhesive tape for stabilizing the cords during the knot tying process. For demonstration purpose, the instructions in this book use pins. With practice, you should be able to tie all designs with bare hands.

A piece of cardboard or corkboard for a work surface.

Be creative with your choice of work surface - even a shoebox could be a great anchor for a knot tying project. Be sure not to poke the pins into anything where you don't want a permanent hole. If you use tape, any smooth surface is fine – desk, table, etc.

Cords vary in their material, shape, and size. They can be cotton, nylon, leather, linen, synthetic silk, or anything else. They can be round, flat, thick, or thin. They can be stiff or soft. Theoretically, you can follow the tutorials and make your bracelets with any type of cord. Choose your cords based on the kind of bracelet you like.

For beginners, a wide cord is easiest to work with. Usually, the cord should be neither too stiff nor too soft. If the cord is too stiff, the loops will skew; If the cord is too soft, then the design will be limp.

Tutorials in this book use 2mm-wide or 2.2mm-wide Chinese knotting cords.

Tweezers (optional) to pull threads in and out of cramped loops.

Beads and charms (optional) to add color and texture to the design. Combining knots and beads gives your bracelet a nice touch.

the Basic Knot

Every project begins with tying a basic knot, the simple knot you already use everyday when tying your shoelaces. We tie all cord ends into basic knots to prevent fraying.

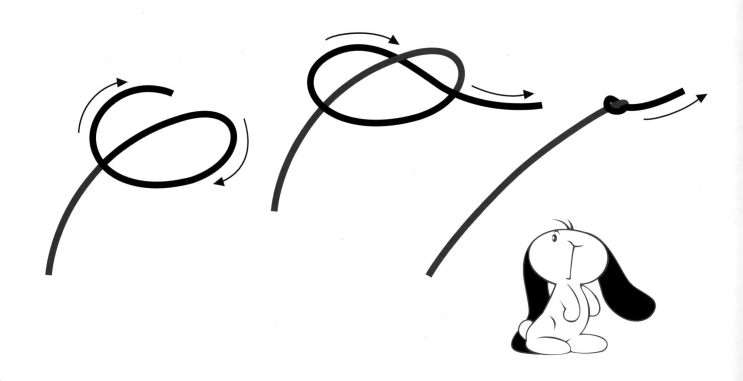

Chapter 5   Simplicity

"Everything should be made as simple as possible, but not simpler."

– Albert Einstein (1879 - 1955)

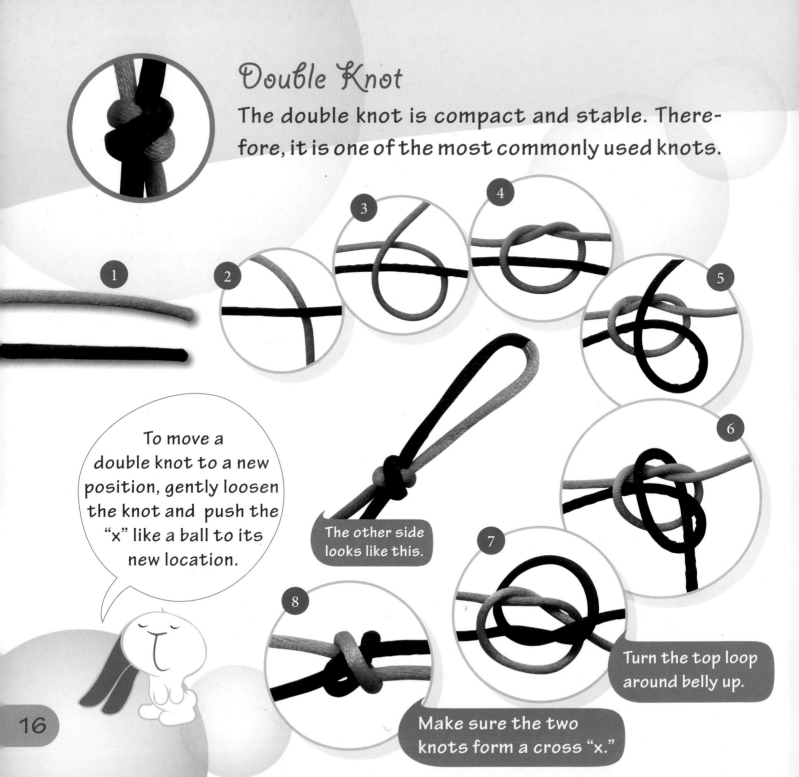

Double Knot

The double knot is compact and stable. Therefore, it is one of the most commonly used knots.

1

2

3

4

5

6

7

Turn the top loop around belly up.

8

Make sure the two knots form a cross "x."

The other side looks like this.

To move a double knot to a new position, gently loosen the knot and push the "x" like a ball to its new location.

16

Helix Knot

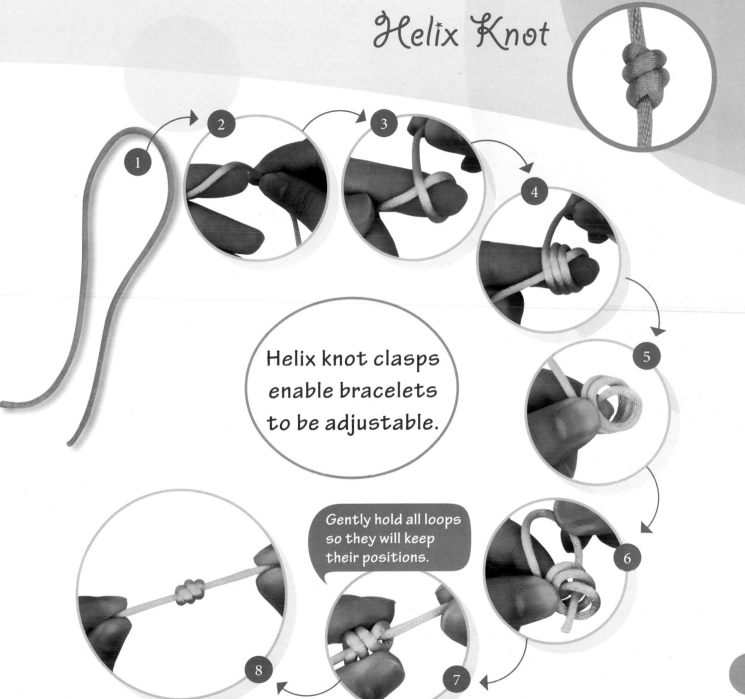

Helix knot clasps enable bracelets to be adjustable.

Gently hold all loops so they will keep their positions.

17

Simplicity Bracelet

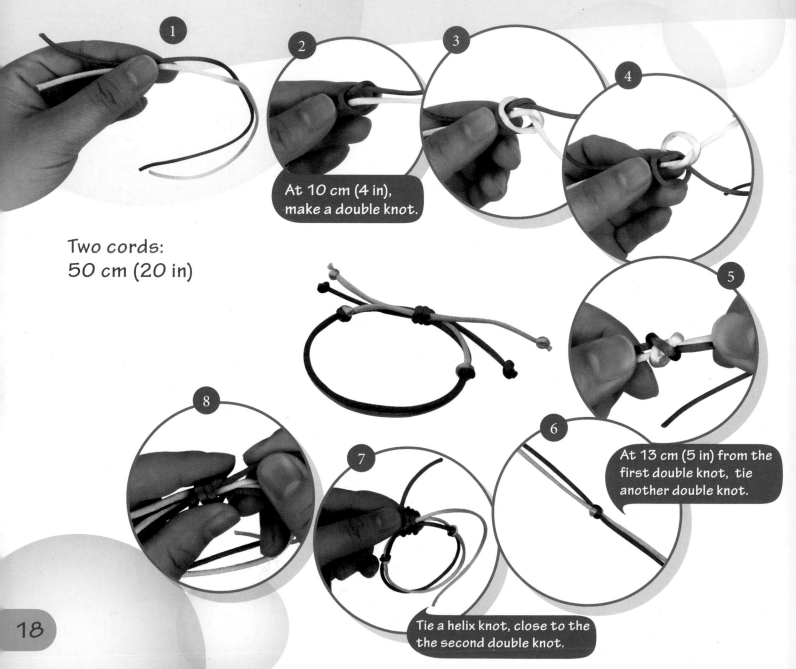

Two cords:
50 cm (20 in)

At 10 cm (4 in), make a double knot.

At 13 cm (5 in) from the first double knot, tie another double knot.

Tie a helix knot, close to the the second double knot.

18

What else can you do with these two knots?

Chapter 6 *Peace*

"Happiness arises in a state of peace, not of tumult."

– Ann Radcliffe (1764 - 1823)

Peace Knot

The Chinese character (平) means "peace." The peace knot is not just a grand wish for world peace, but it is also an auspicious wish for pleasant travels, harmony in marriages, and a healthy life for everyone.

The peace knot is a very simple but beautiful knot because of its symmetry. Western cultures call it a "square knot," or specifically a "reef knot" when sailors use it. It is versatile for color and design combinations, providing much room for your creativity and imagination.

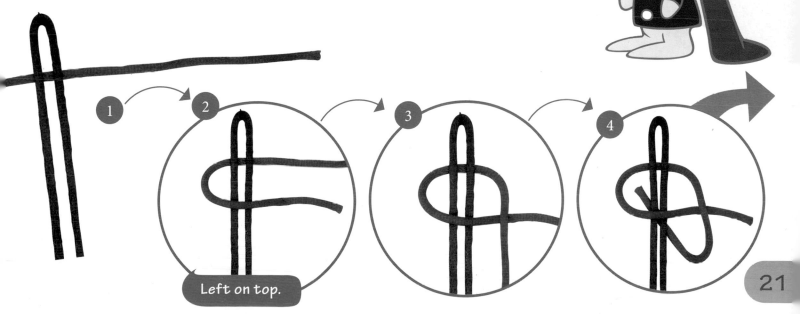

Left on top.

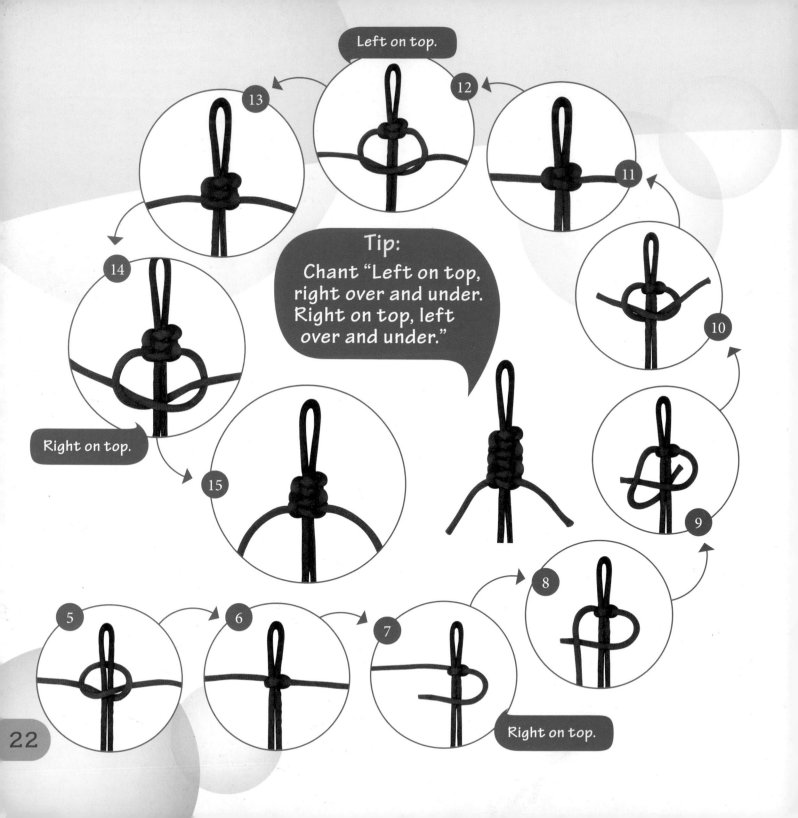

Peace Bracelet

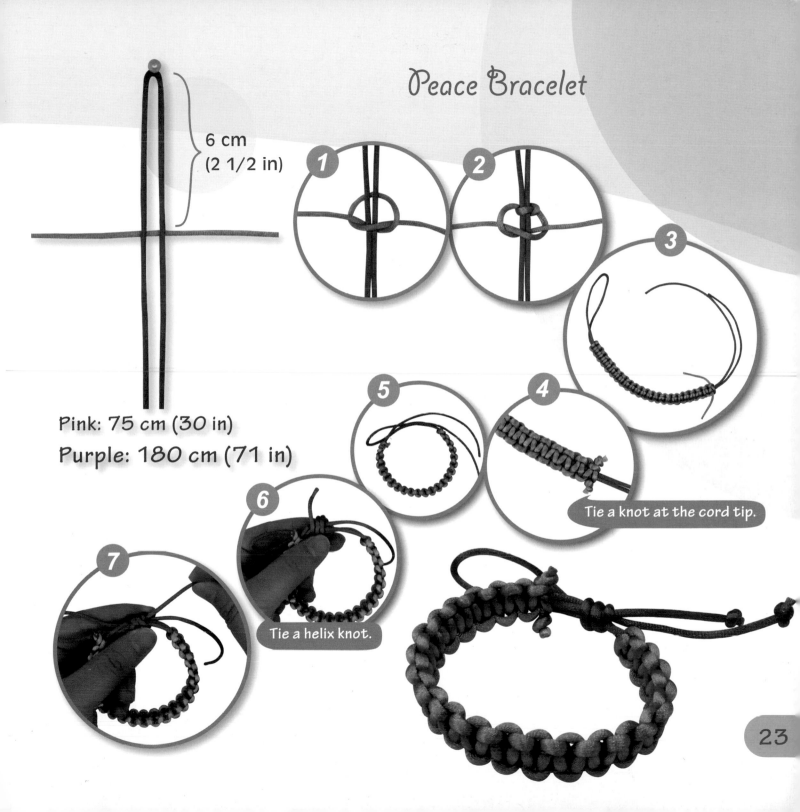

6 cm
(2 1/2 in)

Pink: 75 cm (30 in)
Purple: 180 cm (71 in)

1

2

3

4
Tie a knot at the cord tip.

5

6
Tie a helix knot.

7

Spiral Peace Knot

For a basic peace knot, left and right cords go on top of the axle alternately. You can imagine each cord taking turns to sit on the axle. However, if one cord (either the left or right side) always goes on top, then you will get a spiral peace knot.

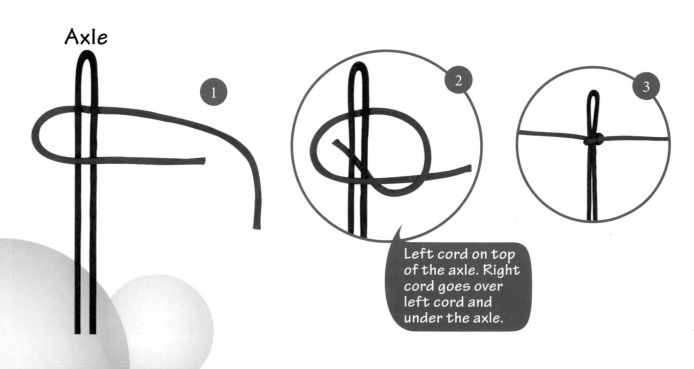

Axle

1

2

3

Left cord on top of the axle. Right cord goes over left cord and under the axle.

24

Spiral Peace Bracelet

Two axle cords: 40 cm (16 in)
Two cords: 90 cm (35 in)

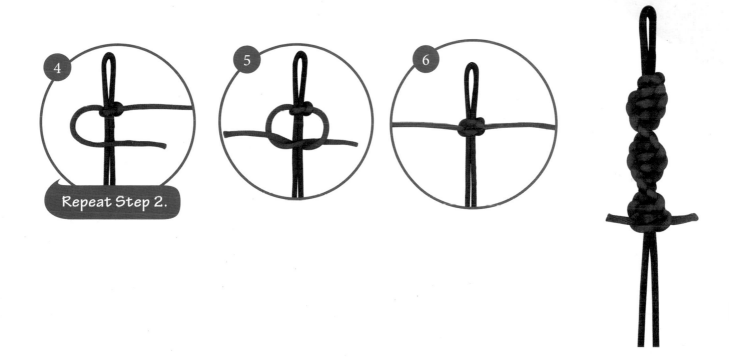

4
Repeat Step 2.

5

6

Dragonfly Bracelet

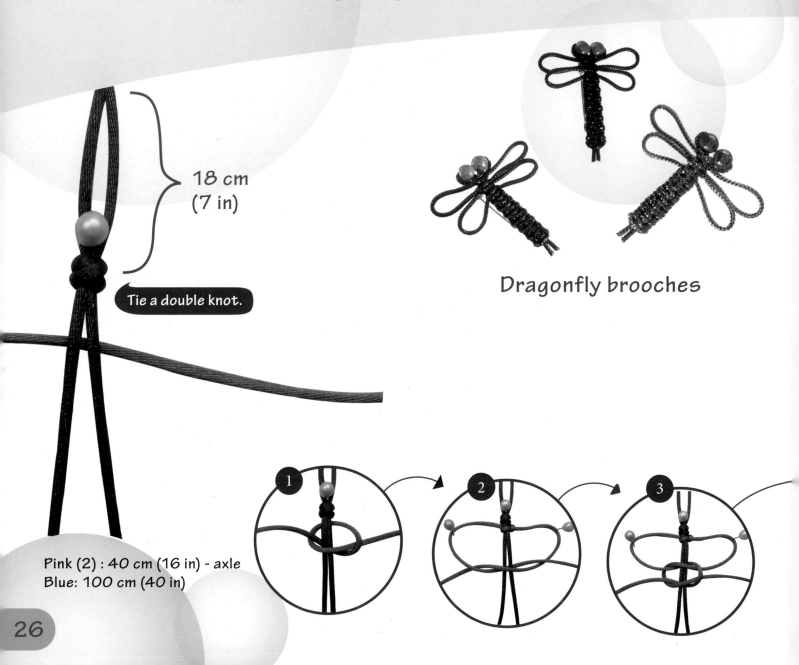

18 cm
(7 in)

Tie a double knot.

Dragonfly brooches

Pink (2) : 40 cm (16 in) - axle
Blue: 100 cm (40 in)

1

2

3

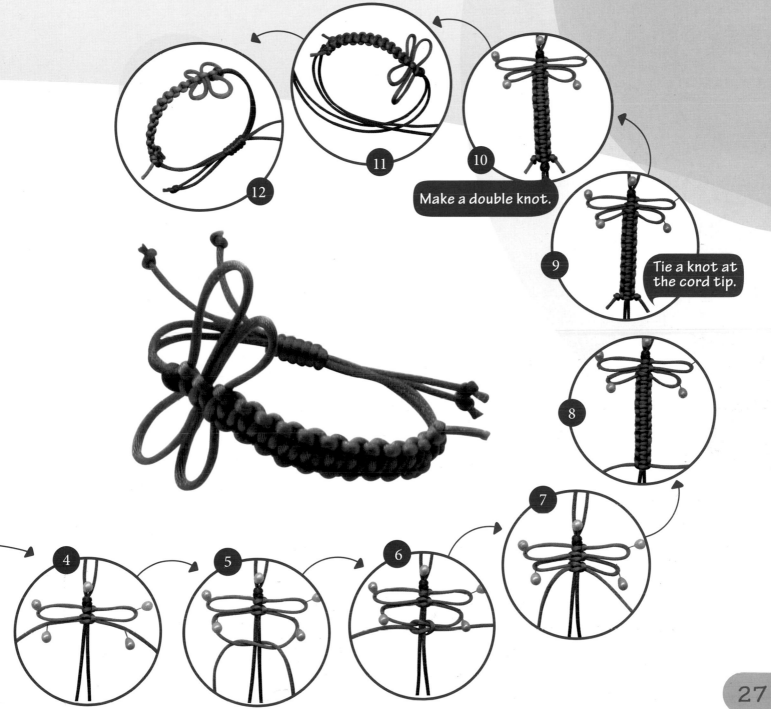

Make a double knot.

Tie a knot at the cord tip.

27

Two-Color Peace Bracelet

Axle cord (2):
40 cm (16 in)

90 cm
(35 in)

90 cm
(35 in)

1

2

3

4

5

6

Cutie Doll

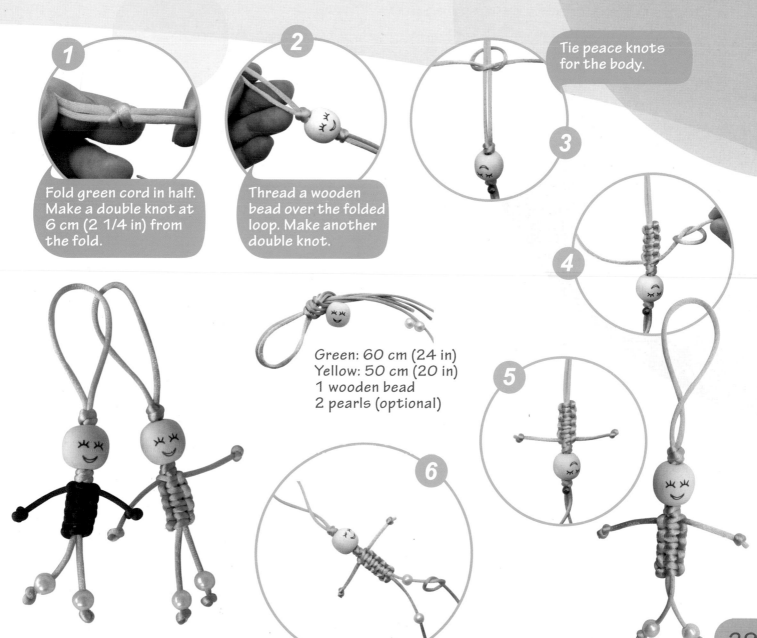

1 Fold green cord in half. Make a double knot at 6 cm (2 1/4 in) from the fold.

2 Thread a wooden bead over the folded loop. Make another double knot.

Tie peace knots for the body.

3

4

5

6

Green: 60 cm (24 in)
Yellow: 50 cm (20 in)
1 wooden bead
2 pearls (optional)

29

Chapter 7   Wealth

"He is richest who is content with the least, for content is the wealth of nature."

– Socrates (469 BC - 399 BC)

"Wealth is not his that has it, but his that enjoys it."

– Benjamin Franklin (1706 - 1790)

Double-Coin Knot

Ancient Chinese coins were circular with a square (or "eye") in the center. This design reflects the ancient Chinese belief that heaven is round and the earth is square. These coins are also called "eye coins," since they reference a Chinese saying that is similar to "before your very eyes." The coin design is a popular wealthbringing motif that merchants hang in front of the door to promote good business. The double-coin knot's shape is like one ancient coin laid on top of another. "Double-coin" is (双钱) in Chinese, a term that sounds like "perfection" or "double completeness" (双全). Thus, the double-coin knot signifies a double blessing.

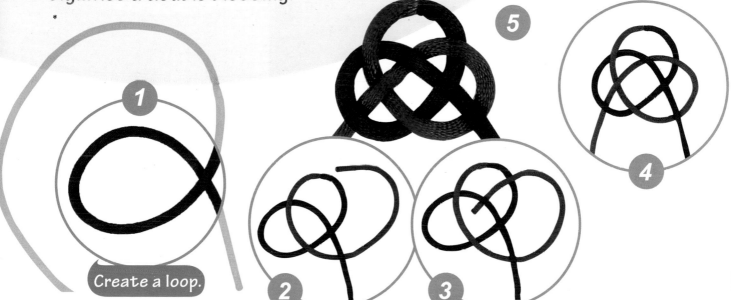

1 Create a loop.

2

3

4

5

Wealth Bracelet

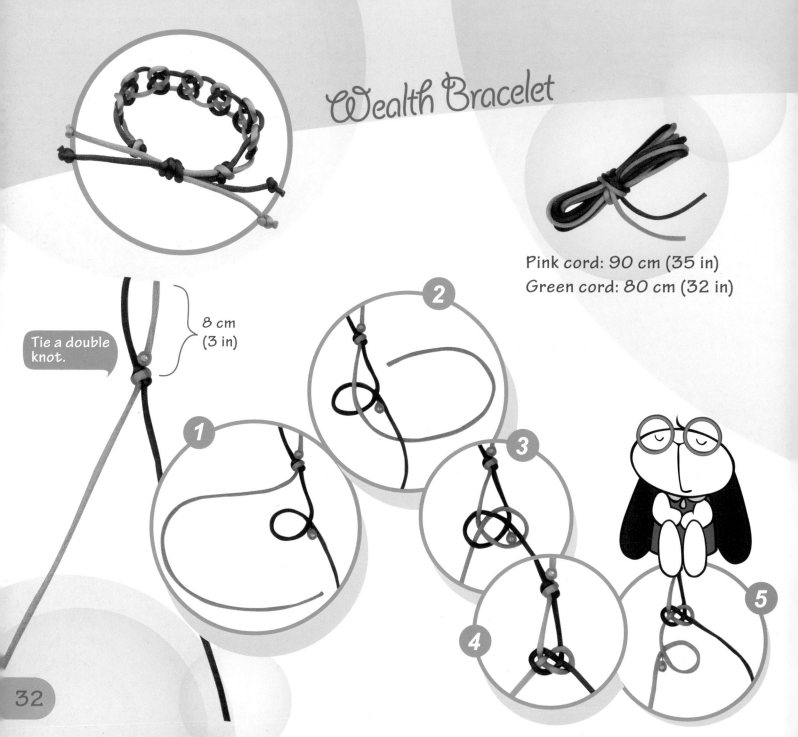

Pink cord: 90 cm (35 in)
Green cord: 80 cm (32 in)

Tie a double knot.

8 cm (3 in)

1

2

3

4

5

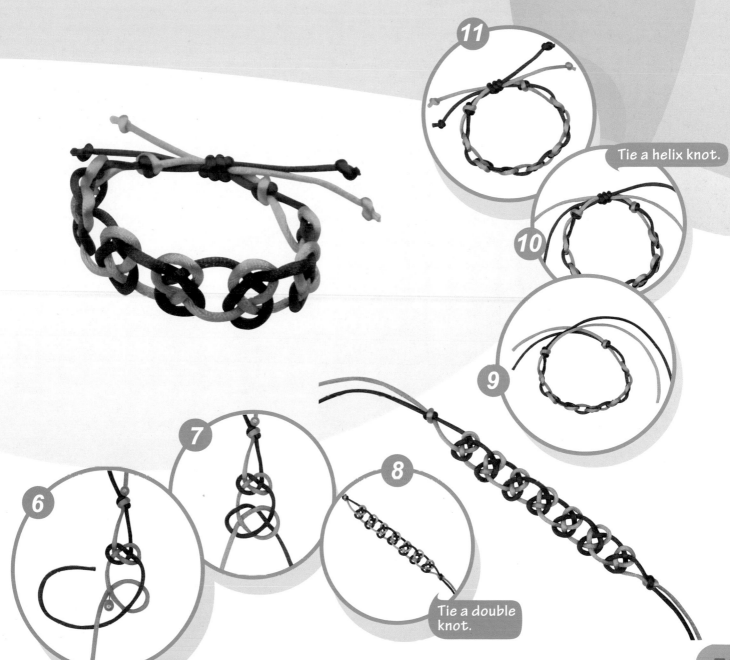

Tie a helix knot.

Tie a double knot.

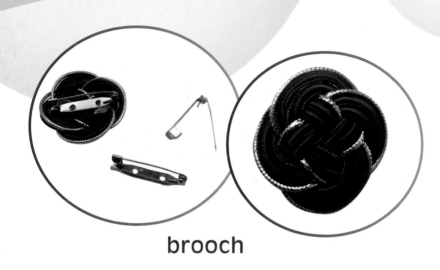

brooch

hair barrette

34

Chapter 8   Friendship

"Friendship improves happiness, and abates misery, by doubling our joys, and dividing our grief."

– Joseph Addison (1672 - 1719)

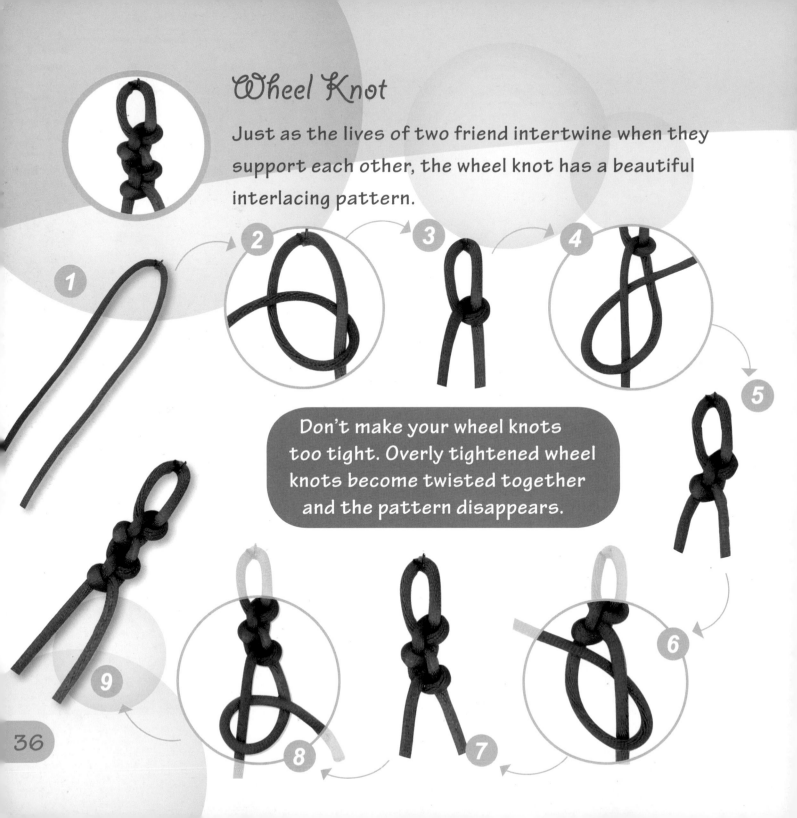

Wheel Knot

Just as the lives of two friend intertwine when they support each other, the wheel knot has a beautiful interlacing pattern.

Don't make your wheel knots too tight. Overly tightened wheel knots become twisted together and the pattern disappears.

36

Hand-in-Hand Friendship Bracelet

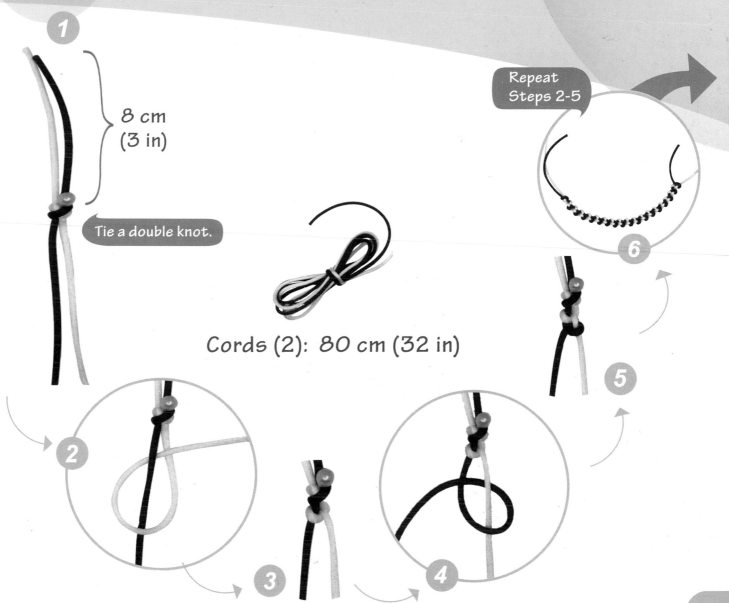

1

8 cm
(3 in)

Tie a double knot.

Cords (2): 80 cm (32 in)

Repeat
Steps 2-5

6

5

2

3

4

Make a
double knot.

38

Creativity at Work

Two-Color Friendship Talisman

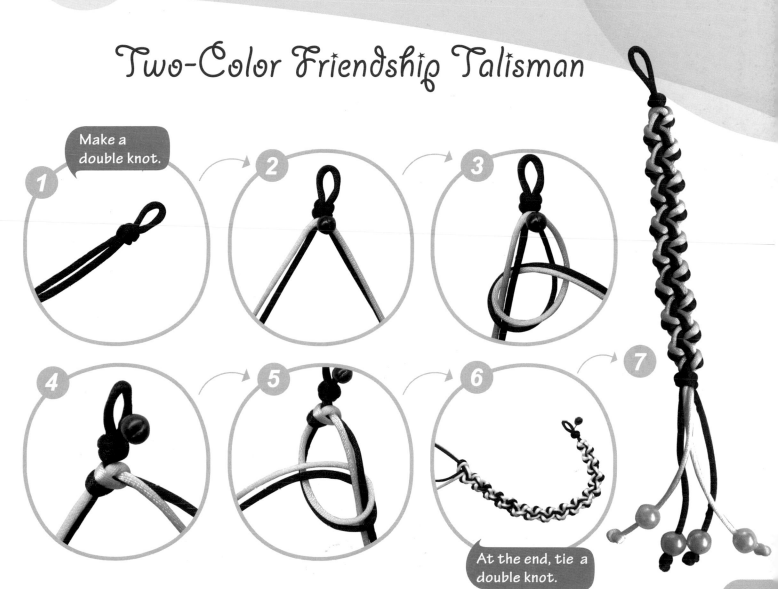

Make a double knot.

1

2

3

4

5

6

7

At the end, tie a double knot.

Chapter 9 Health

"It is health that is real wealth and not
pieces of gold and silver."

– Mohandas Gandhi (1869 - 1948)

Snake Knot

The snake knot is sometimes called a dew knot. The simple interlocking design is customizable with very minor changes. In Western traditions, the snake is often the symbol for healing.

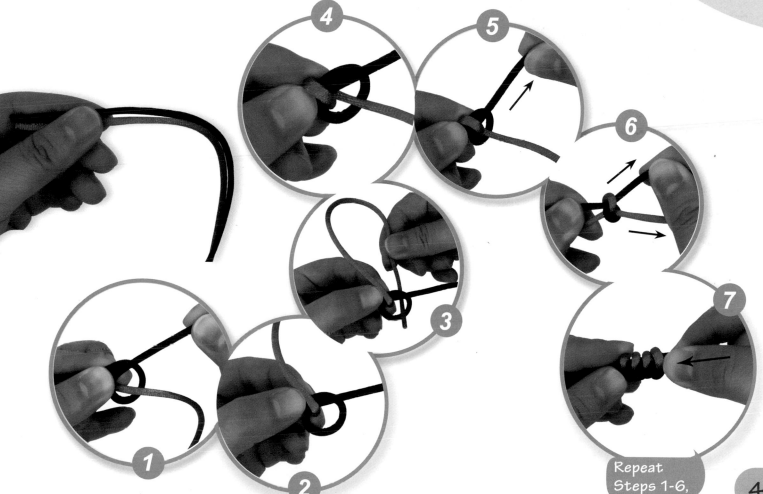

Repeat Steps 1-6,

Health Bracelet

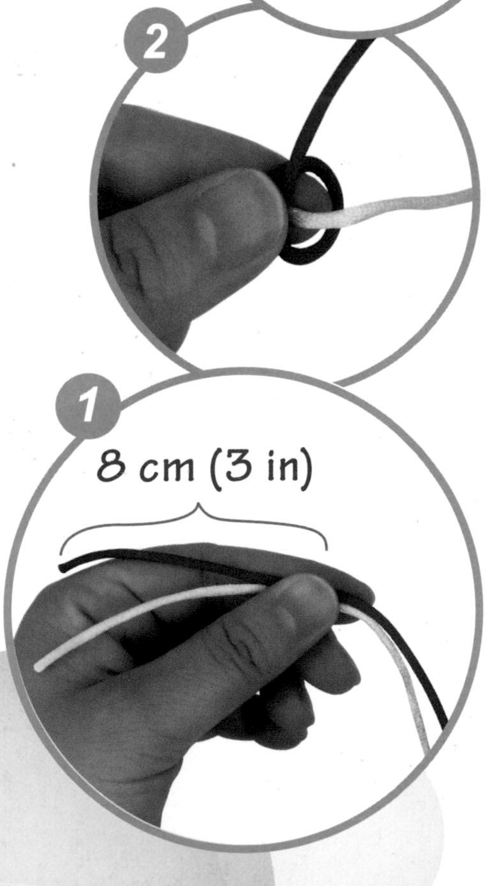

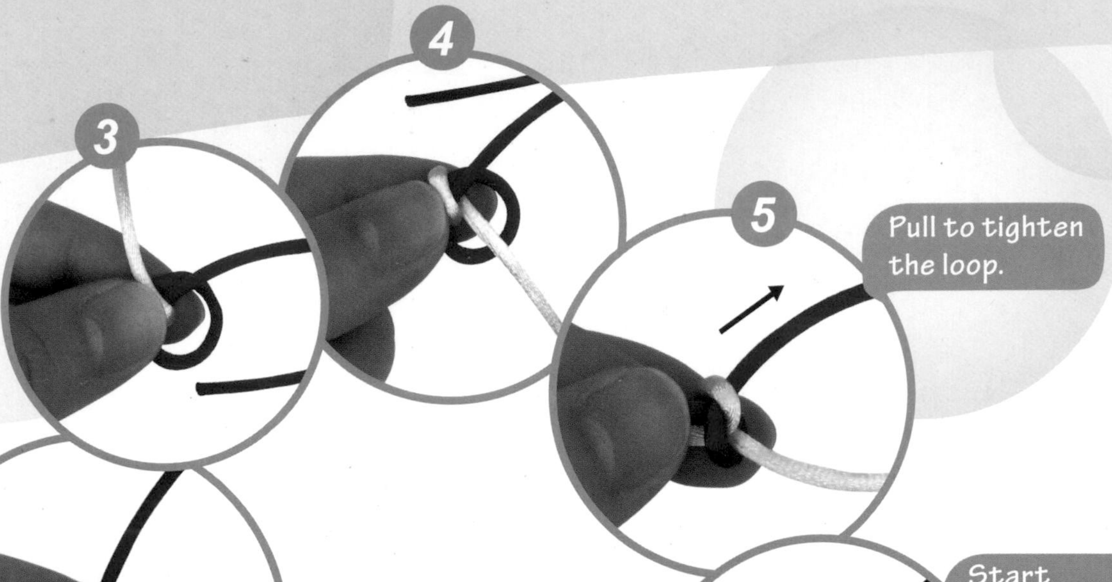

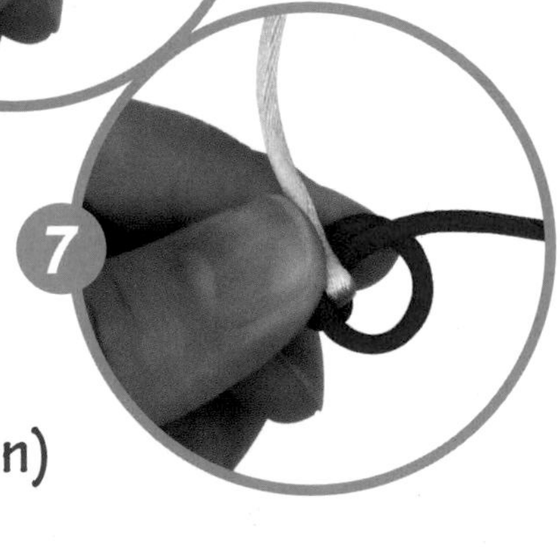

3

4

5

Pull to tighten
the loop.

2

6

Start
another loop.

1

8 cm (3 in)

7

Rosy red: 100 cm (40 in)
Pink: 95 cm (38 in)

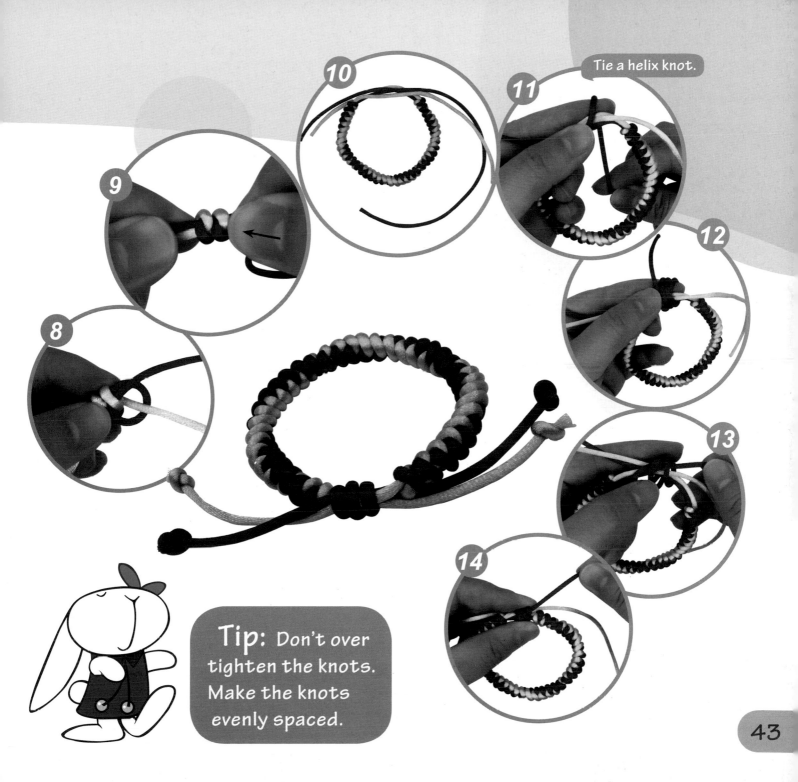

Tie a helix knot.

Tip: Don't over tighten the knots. Make the knots evenly spaced.

43

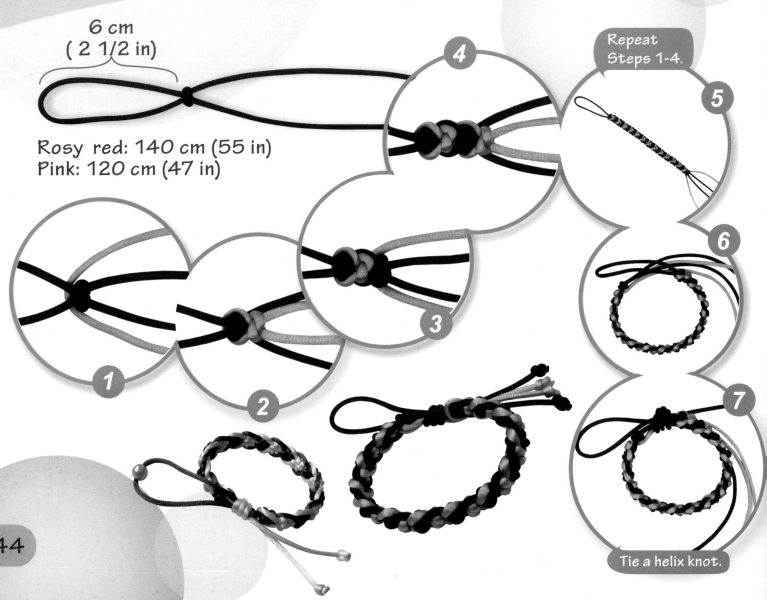

Creativity at Work

Two-Color Health Bracelet

6 cm
(2 1/2 in)

Rosy red: 140 cm (55 in)
Pink: 120 cm (47 in)

1

2

3

4

5

Repeat
Steps 1-4.

6

7

Tie a helix knot.

Chapter 10   Wisdom

"Science is organized knowledge.
Wisdom is organized life."

– Immanuel Kant (1724 - 1804)

Button Knot

The button knot (纽扣) is sometimes called a diamond knot because it resembles the shape of a diamond. In ancient Chinese clothing, the button knot not only was a fastener, but also a beautiful decoration. "纽" is a pictogram of how the belts cross a Chinese traditional garment with a knot that can be untied. In conjunction with double knots, button knots can form a beautiful frog closure button.

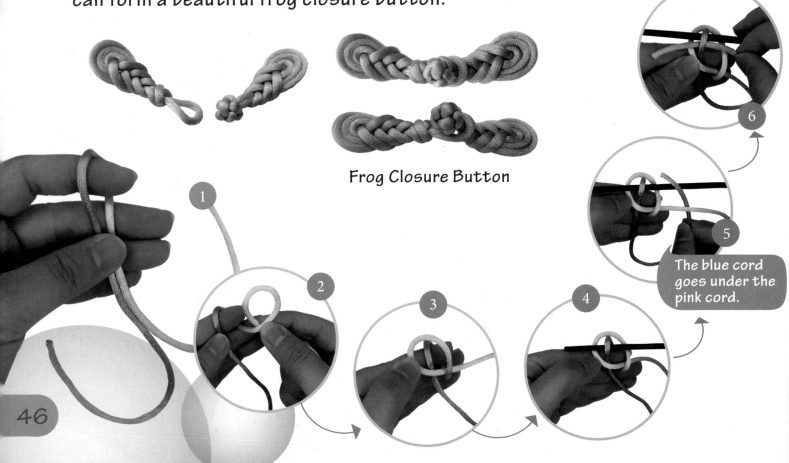

Frog Closure Button

The blue cord goes under the pink cord.

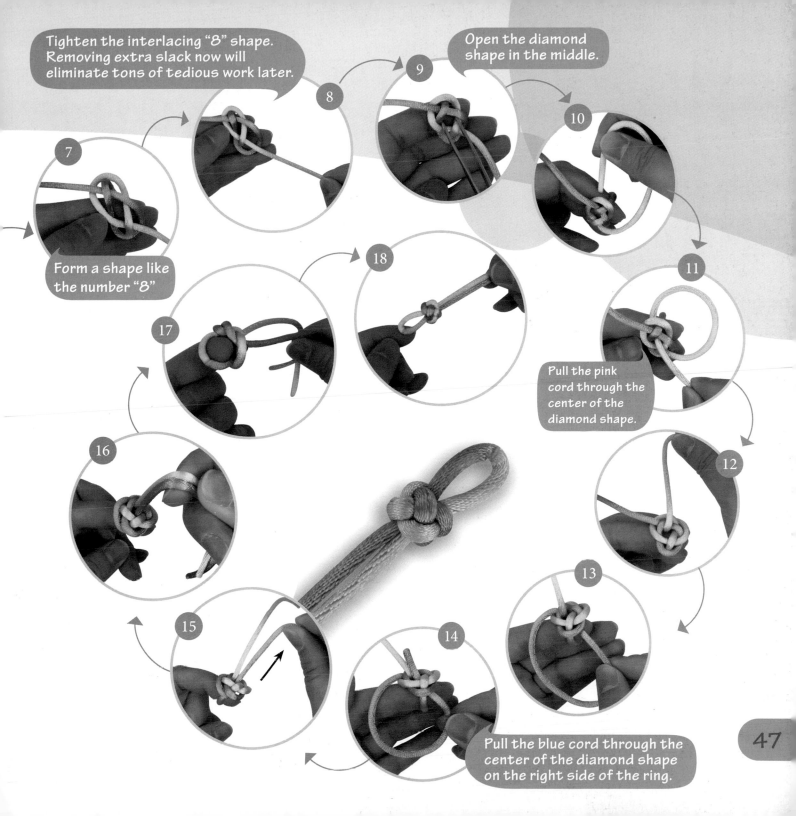

Tighten the interlacing "8" shape. Removing extra slack now will eliminate tons of tedious work later.

Open the diamond shape in the middle.

Form a shape like the number "8"

Pull the pink cord through the center of the diamond shape.

Pull the blue cord through the center of the diamond shape on the right side of the ring.

47

Wisdom Bracelet

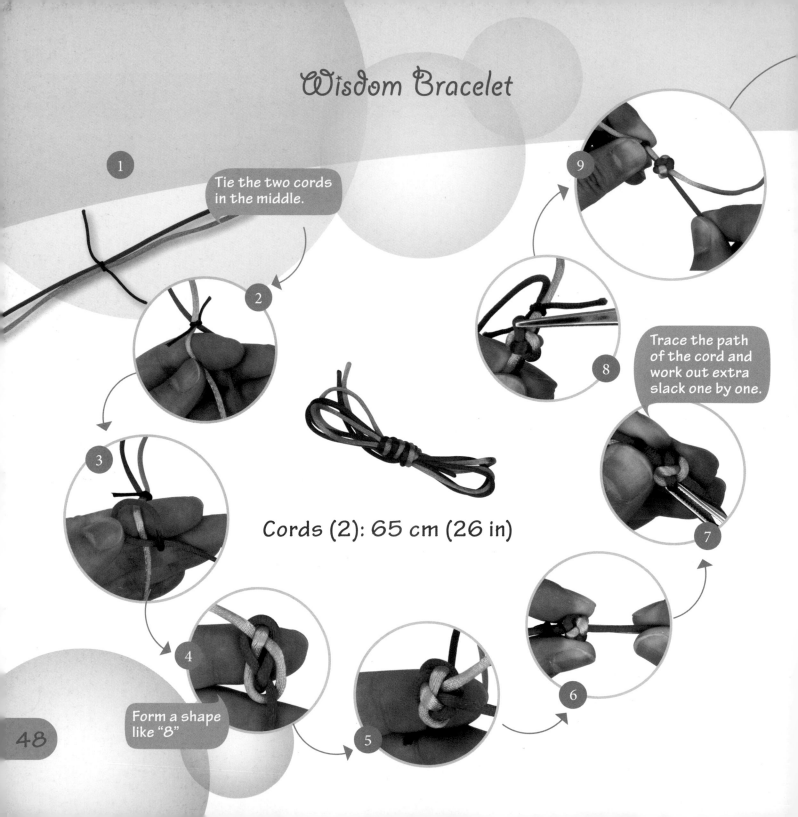

1

Tie the two cords in the middle.

2

3

4

Form a shape like "8"

5

6

7

8

9

Trace the path of the cord and work out extra slack one by one.

Cords (2): 65 cm (26 in)

48

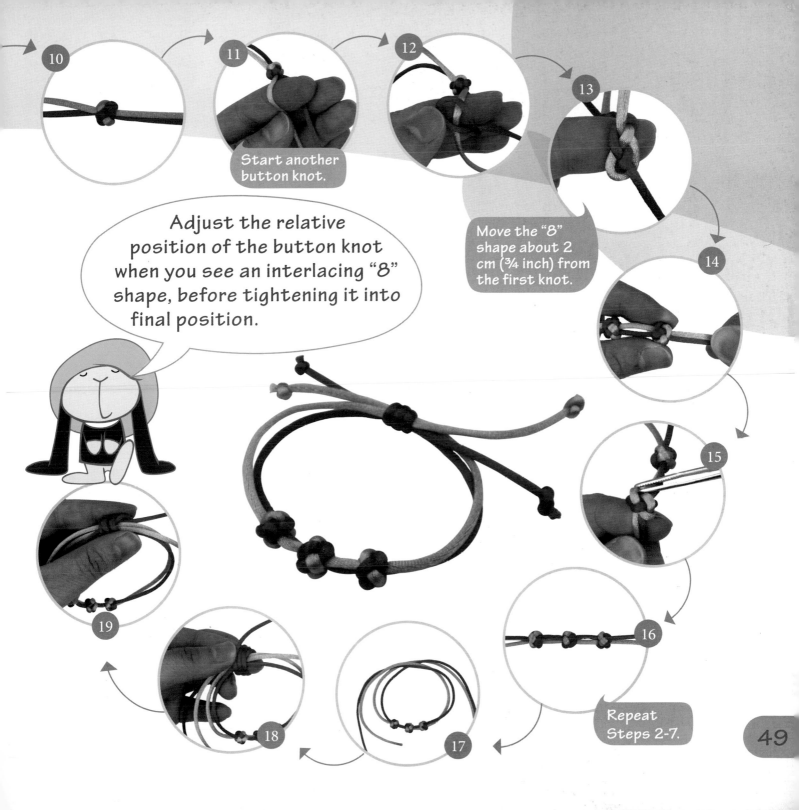

Start another button knot.

Move the "8" shape about 2 cm (¾ inch) from the first knot.

Adjust the relative position of the button knot when you see an interlacing "8" shape, before tightening it into final position.

Repeat Steps 2-7.

49

Creativity at Work

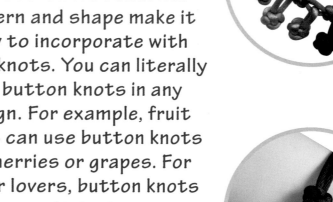

The button knot is very useful. Its beautiful pattern and shape make it easy to incorporate with other knots. You can literally use button knots in any design. For example, fruit lovers can use button knots as cherries or grapes. For flower lovers, button knots can be buds.

Chapter 11   Blessings

"A true friend is the greatest of all blessings, and that which we take the least care of all to acquire."

– Francois de La Rochefoucauld (1613 - 1680)

Cloverleaf Knot

Clover is common in China along roadsides, fields, and yards. Since ancient times, children have enjoyed throwing these delicate greens at each other for fun, pulling each end of a stalk to see which side breaks first, and relishing their fresh and sour taste. Chinese herbalists have created remedies with clover for clearing the throat and it is even used at childbirth.

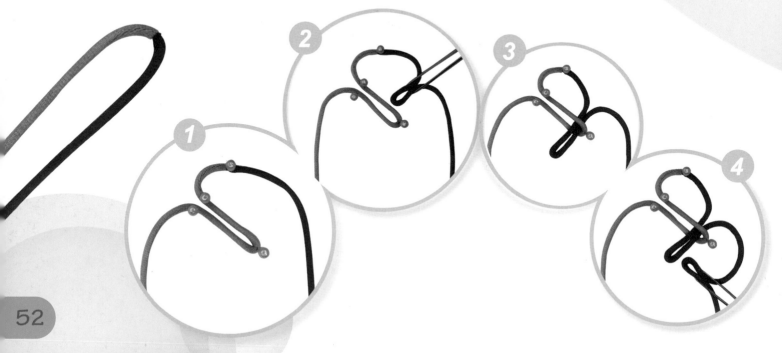

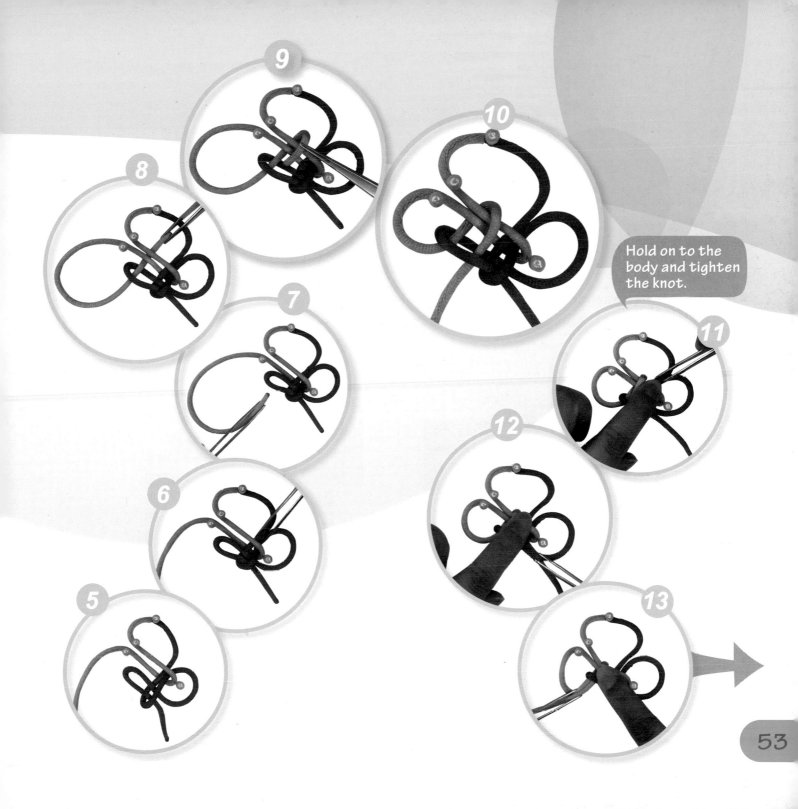

Hold on to the body and tighten the knot.

53

14

15 Take off the pins and hold the knot in your hand.

16 Make sure to hold the knot's body while pulling the cord. Otherwise, the whole knot loosens easily.

17 Shrink each loop one by one.

18

19

20

21

Count-Your-Blessings Bracelet

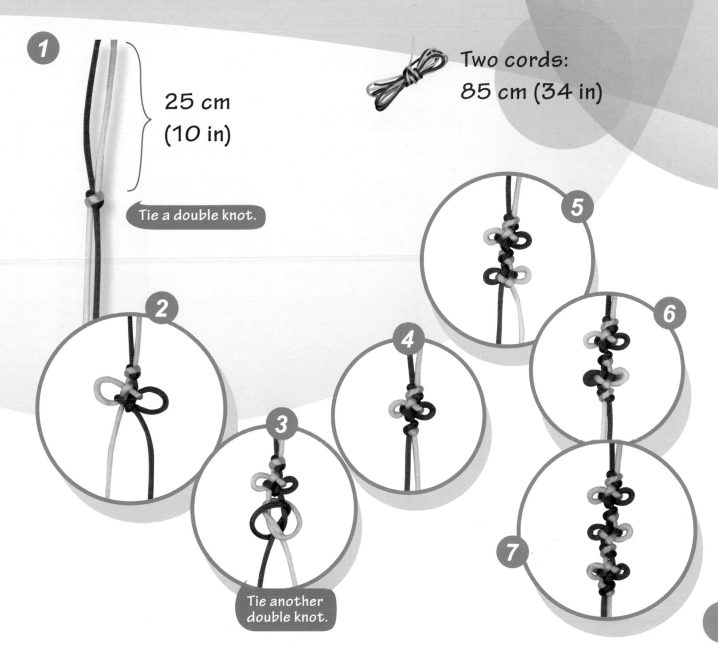

1 25 cm (10 in)

Tie a double knot.

Two cords: 85 cm (34 in)

2

3 Tie another double knot.

4

5

6

7

55

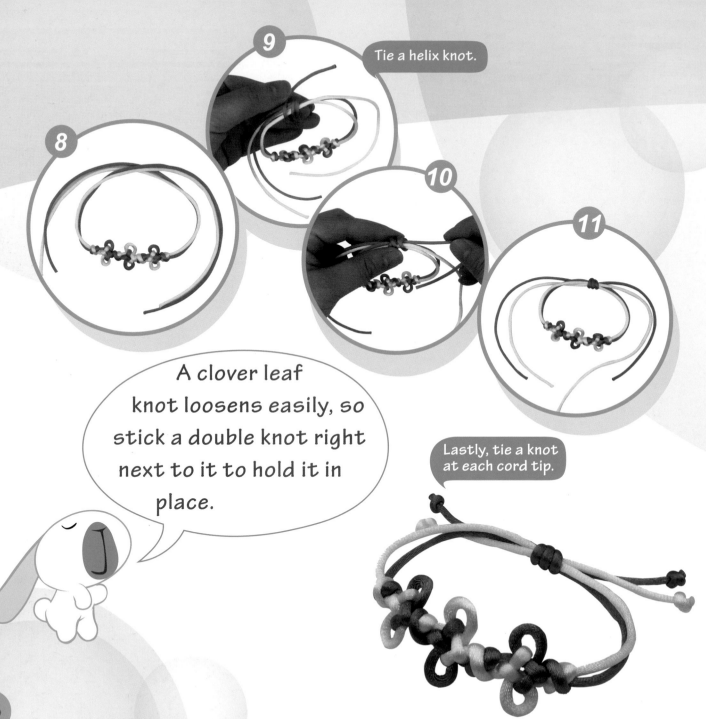

8

9

Tie a helix knot.

10

11

A clover leaf knot loosens easily, so stick a double knot right next to it to hold it in place.

Lastly, tie a knot at each cord tip.

56

Creativity at Work
Bunny-Ear Cloverleaf Knot

Tie two loops instead of three to create
a bunny-ear cloverleaf knot. People often use
the bunny-ear knot to decorate cord-tips.

You can make hundreds of designs with the cloverleaf and bunny-ear knots. The petite floral pattern can form many shapes.

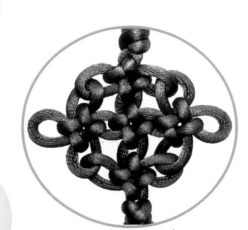

Chapter 12 Luck

"Diligence is the mother of good luck."

– Benjamin Franklin (1706 - 1790)

Lucky Knot

Luck (吉祥) in Chinese is an auspicious, happy word that is usually followed by "anything as you wish." The original lucky knot has exactly seven loops, or ears; therefore it is also called a "seven-loop knot." With some minor alterations, the lucky knot easily transforms into a variety of beautiful floral designs.

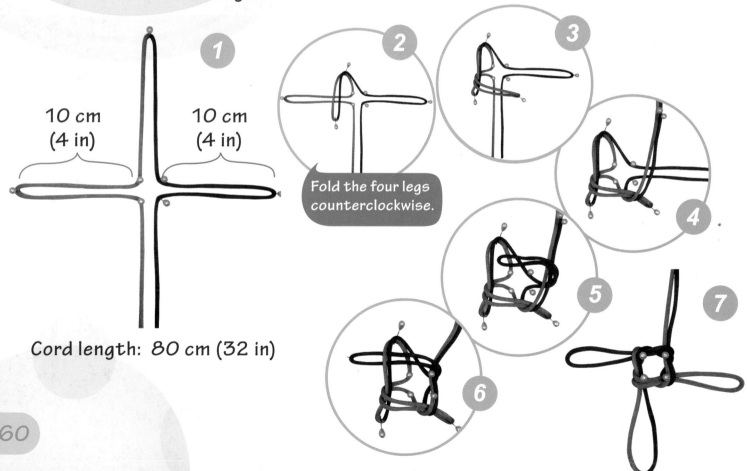

10 cm (4 in)   10 cm (4 in)

Fold the four legs counterclockwise.

Cord length: 80 cm (32 in)

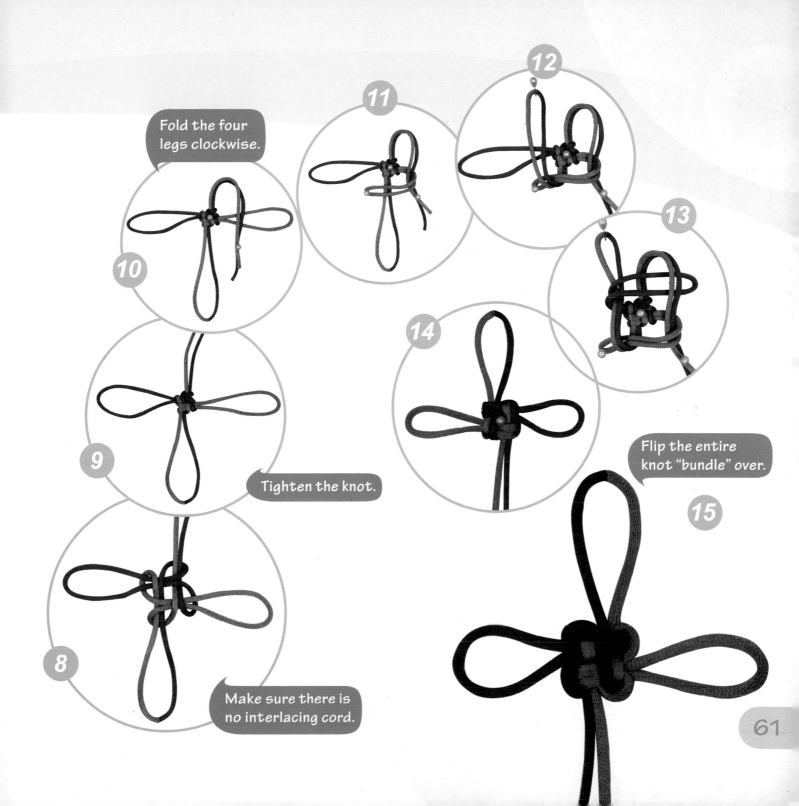

Fold the four legs clockwise.

Tighten the knot.

Flip the entire knot "bundle" over.

Make sure there is no interlacing cord.

61

16

17

18

19

20

21

22

23

24

25

Make minor adjustments.

Lucky Flower Knot

The lucky flower knot is a variation of the lucky knot. The symmetrical shape is beautiful in a bracelet design.

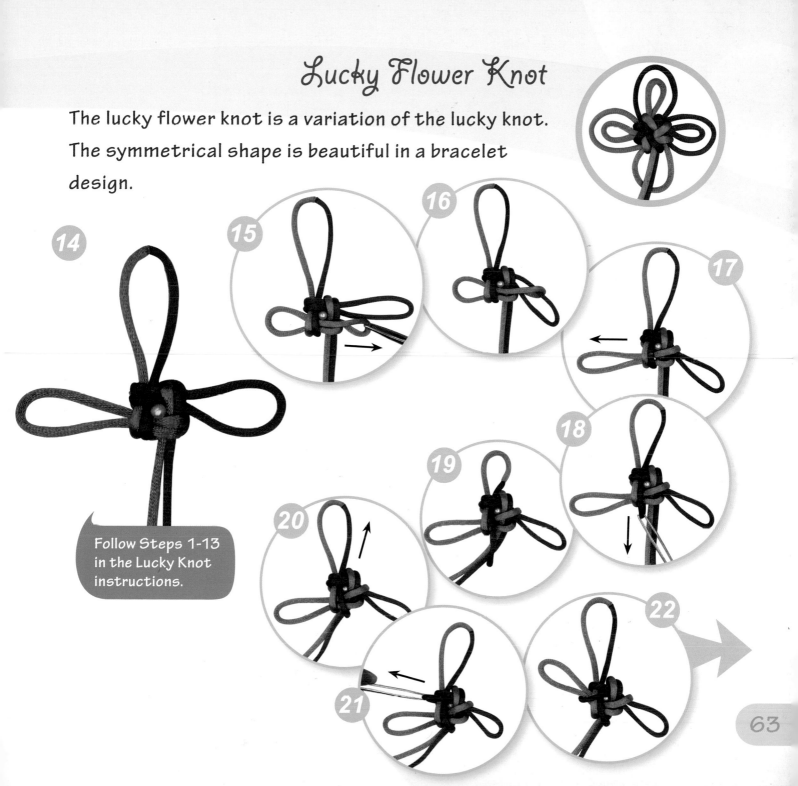

14

Follow Steps 1-13 in the Lucky Knot instructions.

15

16

17

18

19

20

21

22

Lucky Bracelet

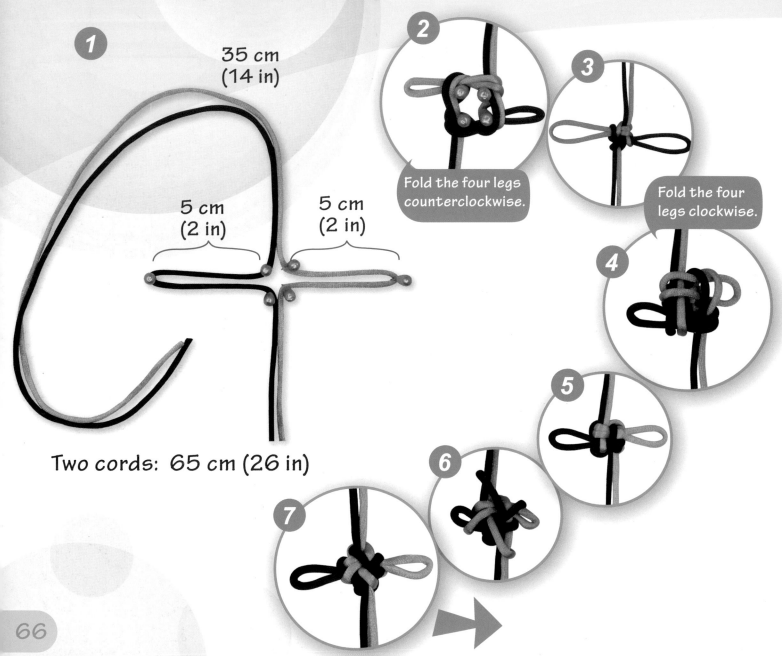

1

35 cm (14 in)

5 cm (2 in)   5 cm (2 in)

Two cords: 65 cm (26 in)

2
Fold the four legs counterclockwise.

3
Fold the four legs clockwise.

4

5

6

7

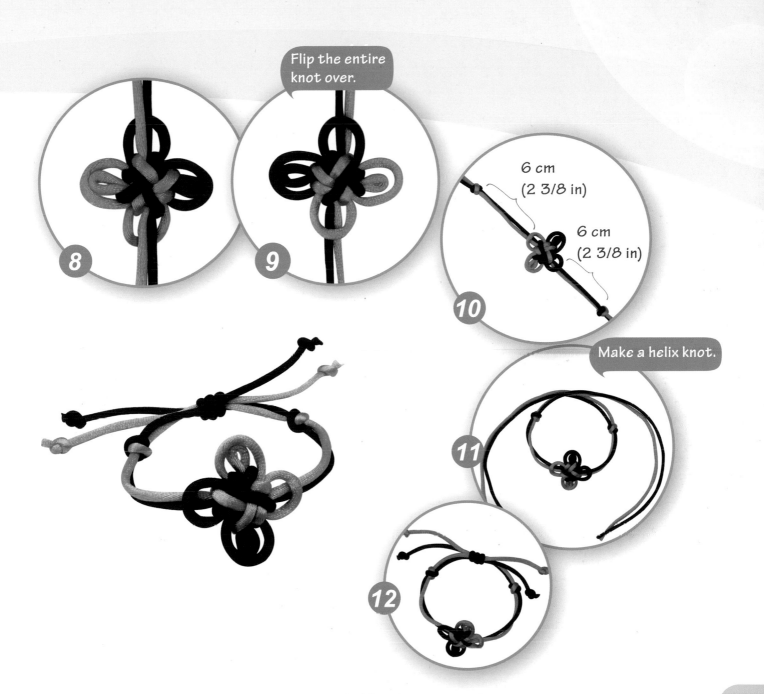

Creativity at Work

The beautiful flower pattern can be made into other decorative hangings.

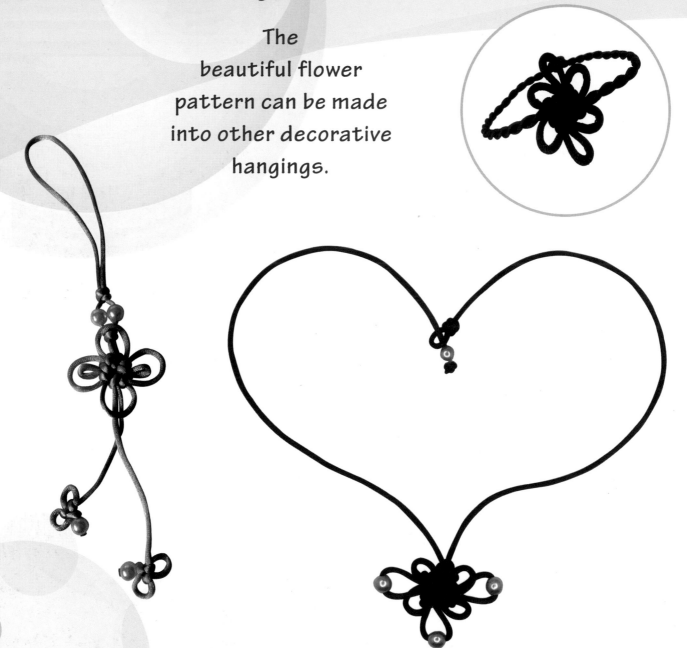

Tip 1: Opening and Closing

There are many ways to create a bracelet clasp. For simplicity, we use a helix knot in this book. However, there are other ways one can create a clasp. We mention two here.

1. Peace Knot

Pros: A truly adjustable clasp with pulls on both sides, unlike the helix knot clasp where only one side is adjustable.

Cons: Unless you know how to seal the cord ends with heat, the clasp is not as clean and neat as a helix knot clasp.

2. Double Knot + Button Knot

In conjunction with a double knot, the button knot is the most common clasp pattern for bracelets, just like the frog button in traditional Chinese dresses and jackets.

Tip 2: Beads and Charms

Create beautiful and fun designs with beads and charms. Sometimes, even just one or two decorative trinkets will add an accent to your bracelets.

About the Authors

D. M. Chen: Lives in sunny California. Chen first became interested in Chinese culture as a child. One day while sitting quietly in a church, she noticed a girl with dexterous fingers transforming a piece of string into a symbolic piece of art. Mesmerized by what she saw, she pursued the art of Chinese knotting and has practiced it ever since. This art form is accessible to children, and Chen advocates that children make these simple but meaningful crafts as gifts for family and friends as a way of avoiding environmentally unfriendly toys.

Michelle Sun: Chinese knotting instructor. Sun loves crafting. At the first sight of Chinese knotting, she immediately fell in love with this type of artwork. However, it wasn't easy at the beginning. One time she tried to make a butterfly. First she was supposed to make the left wing, and later make the right wing. However, she ended up with three left wings and no right wing.

Ready to Tie a Wish?

To help our readers get started, StoryRobin offers a FREE cords package for a limited time, while supplies last.

Become a Robin Island Insider

Sign up for our e-mail newsletter to learn about special offers, contests, games, creative ideas, etc.

Visit **www.storyrobin.com**

FREE

* Actual color combinations are subject to availability.

Visit **www.storyrobin.com**
or
fill out and send us this form.

Who are you?

Name: _____ Age: _____ Boy ○ Girl ○

Address: _____

City: _____ State: _____ Zip: _____

How do you like this book? _____

_____

_____

Email: _____

☐ Check this box if you would like to receive more creative tips from StoryRobin.

Hi, my name is Nicoole.

Tie a Wish™ with Bracelets

 **STORYROBINBOOKS**

Free Cords Offer
P. O. Box 2247
Sunnyvale, CA 94087